THE STORY OF THE

# DENVER

NUGGETS

CREATIVE EDUCATION

Published by Creative Education
123 South Broad Street
Mankato, Minnesota 56001
Creative Education is an imprint of The Creative Company.

DESIGN AND PRODUCTION BY **EVANSDAY DESIGN**

PHOTOGRAPHS BY Associated Press, Getty Images (Brian Bahr,
Bill Baptist / NBAE, Andrew B. Bernstein / NBAE, Jim Cummins /
NBAE, Tim Defrisco / Allsport, Focus on Sport, Andy Hayt / NBAE,
Mike Powell / NBAE, Mary Steinbacher, Rick Stewart / Allsport,
Garrett W. Willwood / NBAE)

**LIBRARY OF CONGRESS CATALOGING-IN-PUBLICATION DATA**

LeBoutillier, Nate.
The story of the Denver Nuggets / by Nate LeBoutillier.
p. cm. — (The NBA—a history of hoops)
Includes index.
ISBN-13: 978-1-58341-405-7
1. Denver Nuggets (Basketball team)—History—
Juvenile literature. I. Title. II. Series.

GV885.52.D46L43 2006
796.323'64'0978883—dc22    2005051205

First edition

9 8 7 6 5 4 3 2 1

COVER PHOTO: *Carmelo Anthony*

# THE STORY OF THE
# DENVER
# NUGGETS

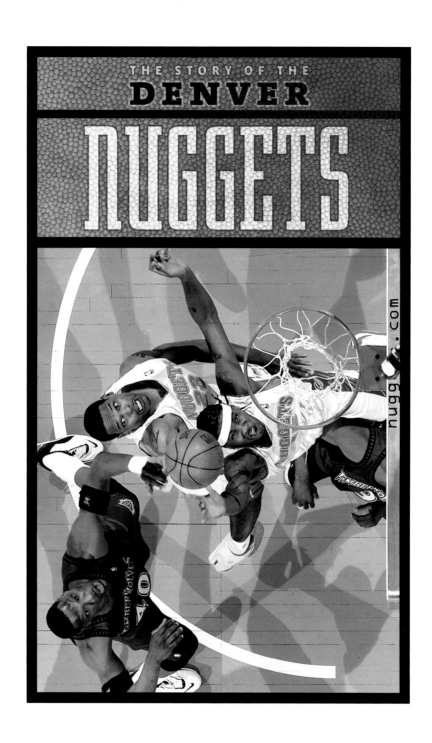

NATE LeBOUTILLIER

CREATIVE EDUCATION

# Everyone in a Nuggets

UNIFORM WAS GOING FULL BLAST. SUPER-FAST SPRINTING, RAPID-FIRE PASSING, AND MACHINE-GUN SHOOTING. THE NUGGETS WEREN'T SO MUCH INTERESTED IN TRYING TO STOP THE OTHER TEAM AS IN TRYING TO OUTSCORE THE OTHER TEAM. THREE-POINTERS, FAST-BREAK LAYUPS, DUNKS, JUMP SHOTS FROM ANYWHERE AT ANY TIME, AND MORE THREE-POINTERS. FANS LOVED THE ACTION, AND PLAYERS GOT A KICK OUT OF THE SYSTEM—NOT TO MENTION A GREAT WORKOUT. DENVER BASKETBALL IN THE 1980S MAY NOT HAVE BEEN ALL THAT SUCCESSFUL IN TERMS OF RAISING CHAMPIONSHIP BANNERS OR HOISTING TROPHIES.

BUT IT SURE WAS FUN.

Denver Colorado

# ROCKETS TO NUGGETS

SETTLED HIGH IN THE FOOTHILLS OF THE ROCKY Mountains, Denver, Colorado, is known as the "Mile High City." Founded by prospectors, the city grew rapidly during the 1870s when large deposits of gold and silver were found nearby. Today, half of all United States coins are minted there, and the city boasts a professional basketball team named for the gold nuggets that put the city on the map—the Denver Nuggets.

The Nuggets started out in 1967 as the Denver Rockets, one of the original teams in the American Basketball Association (ABA). Their first coach was Bob Bass, formerly a successful small-college coach. Forward Wayne Hightower, who had played several seasons in the National Basketball Association (NBA), was Denver's only known star, but the Rockets had a fine first season, finishing 45–33.

9

At a strong and high-flying 6-foot-9, Spencer Haywood was virtually unstoppable as just a rookie

NUGGETS

10

Big guard Ralph Simpson joined Denver's lineup in 1970 and helped turn the Nuggets into an ABA power

A year later, Denver offered a contract to a phenomenal 19-year-old forward named Spencer Haywood. The offer created controversy because Haywood was just a sophomore at the University of Detroit, and there was an unwritten rule that pro teams would not approach college players until they graduated. Haywood's decision to sign with Denver was a groundbreaking move.

In only his first season, Haywood led the league in scoring and rebounding and was named the ABA's Most Valuable Player (MVP). Long-range gunslinging guards Lonnie Wright and Larry Jones helped Haywood fill up the hoop. The Rockets won their division with a 51–33 record and reached the second round of the playoffs. The team also drew big crowds, helping Denver make money at a time when most ABA teams were struggling financially. After playing just one season in Denver, though, Haywood decided to join the NBA's Seattle SuperSonics. Without him, the Rockets fell to last place in 1970–71.

# FIRST DUNK CONTEST

ABA officials were looking for a way to draw a crowd to the 1976 All-Star Game in Denver. The league would soon disband, and it wanted to go out in style. It dawned upon officials that the ABA had some of the best dunkers in the business, including Julius "Dr. J" Erving, David Thompson, and George Gervin. "How about a dunking contest at half-time?" someone asked. It was settled. On January 27, 1976, in Denver, judges scored a collection of dunkers on "artistic ability, imagination, body flow, and fan response." Hometown favorite David "The Skywalker" Thompson impressed fans with a double-pump reverse jam. But contest winner Dr. J stole the show. Launching himself from the free-throw line, Dr. J flew 15 feet and slammed the ball through the rim. The crowd went wild.

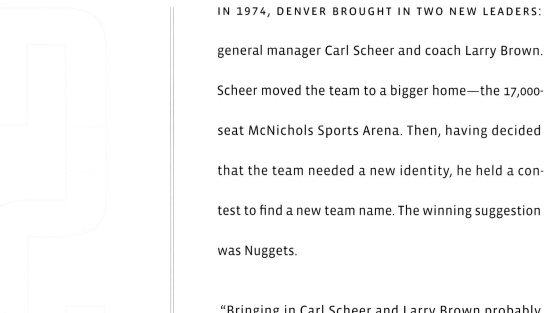

IN 1974, DENVER BROUGHT IN TWO NEW LEADERS: general manager Carl Scheer and coach Larry Brown. Scheer moved the team to a bigger home—the 17,000-seat McNichols Sports Arena. Then, having decided that the team needed a new identity, he held a contest to find a new team name. The winning suggestion was Nuggets.

 "Bringing in Carl Scheer and Larry Brown probably saved the Denver franchise…," said Nuggets center Dave Robisch. "There was serious apathy about the basketball club. We lost our first game [in 1974–75], and nobody seemed to notice. But when we won our next nine in a row, people starting packing the arena, and we became the hottest ticket in town."

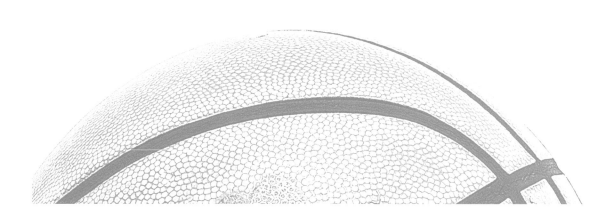

NUGGETS

Denver star David Thompson was among the most electrifying performers of the ABA's nine-year run

14

Dan Issel, who would later coach the Nuggets, averaged 20 points a game across his Denver career

The Nuggets earned Denver's attention for good reason. The team that had gone 37–47 the previous season suddenly seemed unstoppable, jumping to an ABA-record 65–19 mark. Coach Brown had assembled a talented lineup that was led by guard Mack Calvin, a great ball handler. Ralph Simpson teamed up with Calvin in the backcourt, while big men Byron Beck, Dave Robisch, and rookie Bobby Jones anchored the frontcourt.

The Nuggets lost to the Indiana Pacers in the 1975 playoffs but drafted David Thompson in the off-season. With Thompson—a swingman nicknamed "The Skywalker" because of his amazing jumping ability—on board, the excitement rose even higher in Denver. The Nuggets had also traded for forward Dan Issel, one of the hardest-working players in the league. Known as "The Horse," he was a tough rebounder and a steady scorer.

Denver posted the ABA's best record again in 1975–76 with a 60–24 mark. The Nuggets drove as far as the league finals before falling to "Dr. J" (Julius Erving) and the New York Nets. It was to be the ABA's final championship. By 1976, the ABA was in trouble. Attendance was generally low, and the league had been unable to land a national television contract. Still, the league had some of the game's best players, so the NBA decided to add the ABA's top four teams. Denver was among them.

## GOOD COACH, BAD DRESSER

Most NBA coaches dress in linen suits and ties. Doug Moe, Denver's head coach from 1980 to 1990, wore wrinkled cotton and a red blazer. Or a purple shirt with a maroon jacket. Or a checkered-print suit with ratty tennis shoes. When asked to comment on his choice of apparel, Moe replied, "Am I in a beauty contest or something? I wasn't put on this Earth to look good or impress anybody." When asked why he did not always wear a tie, he said, "I've never been comfortable with a tie. In my mind, ties are ridiculous for a coach to wear. This is an emotional business." Moe's affection for ugly clothes did not affect the way his players and Nuggets fans felt about him, though. He remains one of Denver's most beloved coaches.

17

McNichols Sports Arena was the home of the Nuggets for 24 seasons and hosted 47 playoff games

NUGGETS

# DENVER GOES WITH MOE

THE NUGGETS PROVED THAT THEY BELONGED AMONG the NBA's best by going 50–32 and winning the Midwest Division in 1976–77. But Larry Brown stepped down as coach in 1978, and Denver faded in the standings. In 1979–80, the Nuggets went 30–52. The season's only highlight was the addition of Alex English, a high-scoring guard previously with the Indiana Pacers.

After the Nuggets got off to a slow start the next year, former assistant coach Doug Moe took the head coaching reins. Moe was known for his sarcastic sense of humor and wide-open style of offense. "Moe had no set plays, ran short practices that were primarily conditioning drills, and told his players to shoot whenever they wanted," noted NBA writer Zander Hollander.

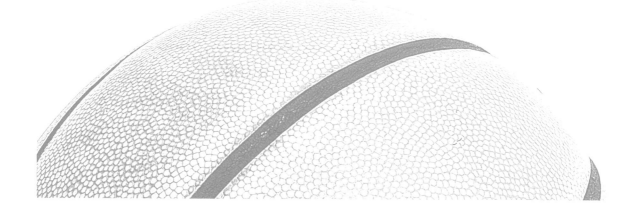

NUGGETS

Graceful sharpshooter Alex English led Denver to the playoffs for nine straight seasons in the 1980s

Rocky Mountain News

Fan favorite Fat Lever earned All-Star honors twice (1987–88 and 1989–90) in the Mile High City

NUGGETS

With the offense-minded Moe in control, Thompson, English, Issel, and forward Kiki Vandeweghe all burned up the nets throughout the early 1980s. Unfortunately, the Nuggets' defense was porous. In 1983–84, Denver once scored 184 points in a game—and still lost (186–184 to Detroit). Fans packed McNichols Arena, but the team was ousted early from the play-offs every year.

In 1984, the Nuggets sent the high-scoring Vandeweghe to Portland for three players, including guard Lafayette "Fat" Lever. The reshaped Nuggets lineup went 52–30 and drove all the way to the Western Conference Finals in 1985 before losing to the Los Angeles Lakers. Lever, especially, gave the Nuggets valuable leadership. "Fat Lever has all of these 'plus' factors," said Dallas Mavericks coach Richie Adubato. "[He's a] fierce competitor, best rebounding guard in the league, great defensive player, great assist man, and good scorer."

The Nuggets stormed back with a 54–28 record in 1987–88. Part of their success was due to newcomer Michael Adams. The 5-foot-9 guard, obtained in a trade with the Washington Bullets, had great speed and was a terrific defender. He also accurately launched scores of three-point bombs with an unconventional, one-handed push shot. Still, the Nuggets leveled off as a mediocre team in the late 1980s.

## HISTORICALLY HIGH SCORING

Coach Doug Moe pushed offense. *Sprint to the basket and shoot, shoot, shoot!* was Moe's philosophy. His Nuggets certainly proved they could score points on December 13, 1983, when they were beaten 186–184 by the Detroit Pistons in the NBA's highest-scoring game ever. The Pistons' Isiah Thomas scored 47 points, John Lang scored 41, and Kelly Tripucka scored 35, while high scorers for the Nuggets were Kiki Vandeweghe with 51 points and Alex English with 47. "Oh, it was great," said English, commenting on the Nuggets' free-shooting days. "That was basketball at its finest. People talk about us not playing defense and all the points, but now the league is trying to get back to it, the excitement. We weren't really the pioneers, but we were one of the best at it."

23

Despite his short stature guard Michael Adams found ways to score from both long and close range

NUGGETS

IN 1990, A NEW GROUP OF OWNERS TOOK OVER the Nuggets, and changes followed. English left town as a free agent, Lever was traded away, and Moe stepped down as coach. These changes resulted in an NBA-worst 20–62 record in 1990–91.

In the 1991 NBA Draft, the Nuggets selected 7-foot-2 center Dikembe Mutombo. Although his offensive skills were unspectacular, "Mount Mutombo" excelled in other ways. "Son," John Thompson—who coached Mutombo at Georgetown University—told Mutombo, "you will make millions and millions of dollars more than people who score if you can play defense, which means two things—rebounding and blocking shots."

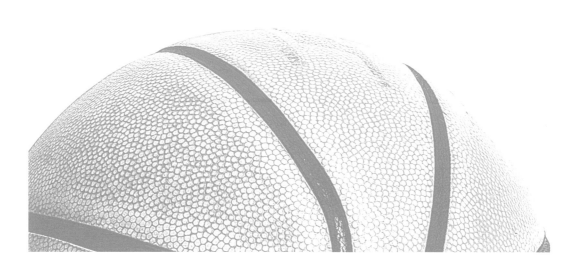

25

NUGGETS

Dikembe Mutombo owns Denver franchise records for the most rebounds (31) and blocks (12) in a game

Antonio McDyess spent two seasons in Denver, one in Phoenix, then four more with the Nuggets

With former Nuggets great and local hero Dan Issel as head coach, Mutombo, veteran guard Bryant Stith, and point guard Mahmoud Abdul-Rauf—another young player drafted in the early '90s—led Denver to a franchise highlight in the 1994 playoffs. The Nuggets faced the Seattle SuperSonics, owners of the NBA's best record, in a best-of-five series. Seattle won the first two games, but Mutombo dominated the paint in the next three as Denver pulled off one of the biggest playoff series upsets in NBA history.

Mutombo and Abdul-Rauf led the team over the next few seasons with the help of talented young forward Antonio McDyess. With long arms, a muscular build, and great leaping ability, the 6-foot-9 McDyess was capable of dominating players of all sizes at both ends of the floor.

Still, the Nuggets posted a mediocre record in 1995–96, and Issel resigned at midseason. One by one, Denver's stars then left town. Mutombo signed with the Atlanta Hawks, and Abdul-Rauf and McDyess were traded away. Without their three best players, the Nuggets fell apart. In 1997–98, they posted an embarrassing 11–71 record.

# BASKETBALL, FAITH, AND PATRIOTISM

Denver Nuggets fans became irritated. They called in to radio shows and complained. They wrote letters and e-mails to sports television programs. They discussed it at concession stands. They could not figure out why their point guard would not stand for the "Star-Spangled Banner." Mahmoud Abdul-Rauf (formerly known as Chris Jackson), refused to stand during the United States' National Anthem when it was played before games during the 1996–97 season. Abdul-Rauf said that his Islamic faith forbade him from standing for any "nationalistic ideology." Said Abdul-Rauf, "My beliefs are more important than anything." After two games, though, the NBA intervened and suspended him until he stood "in a dignified posture." Abdul-Rauf agreed to stand during the anthem and "offer a prayer, my own prayer, for those who are suffering."

## CARMELO AND THE NEW NUGGETS

IN 1999–00, THE NUGGETS PLAYED in A NEW HOME: Denver's state-of-the-art Pepsi Center. Dan Issel returned for a second stint as coach, guiding his young team to an improved record. But Issel wouldn't stay long, stepping down in 2001. The Nuggets declined again, dipping to 17–65 in 2002–03.

Desperate for some new stars, the Nuggets picked up forward Carmelo Anthony, fresh off a collegiate national championship at Syracuse University, with the third pick of the 2003 NBA Draft. Anthony, along with new additions such as point guard Andre Miller, 5-foot-5 guard "Little" Earl Boykins, and center Marcus Camby, led the 2003–04 Nuggets to an amazing turnaround. They went 43–39 and made it into the playoffs for the first time in nine seasons.

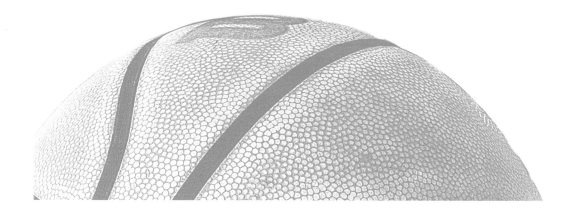

29

A 6-foot-8 forward with endless skill, Carmelo Anthony entered the NBA with sky-high expectations

NUGGETS

TOP DOG

Forward Kenyon Martin gave the rebuilt Nuggets lineup speed, toughness, and an aggressive attitude

Denver's rise continued in 2004–05. The acquisition of tough forward Kenyon Martin, a forward who had played in two NBA Finals with the New Jersey Nets, sent the Nuggets' stock soaring in the summer of 2004. But the team got off to a disappointing 17–25 start and hired new coach George Karl at midseason.

Coach Karl turned the team around. Following his call for an all-out offensive attack—similar to Denver teams of the 1980s—the Nuggets won 32 of their final 40 games and bounded into the playoffs. They stunned the eventual champion San Antonio Spurs in Game 1 of their opening-round series but lost the next four. Still, with Karl at the helm and a talented lineup in place, the Nuggets' prospects were looking up. Said Coach Karl of his plan for the Nuggets, "Personally, I would like to play fast, faster, and fastest."

The Nuggets are clearly going back to running and gunning. While the Nuggets of the 1980s were entertaining, championship-level success was hard to come by. Today's Nuggets plan to both entertain their devoted fans *and* add the precious metal of a league championship trophy to the Mile High City.

## ALEX ENGLISH—NUGGETS CLASSIC

A lithe, 6-foot-7 forward exploded on the court for the Nuggets in February 1980. His name was Alex English, and over the next 11 seasons, he would play in eight All-Star games and score 21,645 points, tops in Nuggets history. But in 1989–90, the 36-year-old's average fell to 17.9 points per game, and the Nuggets did not re-sign him. English was disappointed. "I had envisioned that I would go out like Dan Issel and Julius Erving," English said, "that I would make the trip around the league and get to say good-bye to all the people in all the different cities." English played one season with the Dallas Mavericks and one season in Italy before retiring as the seventh-leading scorer in NBA history. In 1992, Denver apologized to English and retired his uniform.